A Con
Introdu
to Gl

i

ALSO AVAILABLE

A Concise Introduction to GEM

by
J. W. Penfold

BERNARD BABANI (publishing) LTD.
THE GRAMPIANS
SHEPHERDS BUSH ROAD
LONDON W6 7NF
ENGLAND

PLEASE NOTE

Although every care has been taken with the production of this book to ensure that any project, designs, modifications and/or programs etc. contained herewith, operate in a correct and safe manner and also that any components specified are normally available in Great Britain, the Publishers and Author do not accept responsibility in any way for the failure, including fault in design, of any project, design, modification or program to work correctly or to cause damage to any other equipment that it may be connected to or used in conjunction with, or in respect of any other damage or injury that may be so caused, nor do the Publishers accept responsibility in any way for the failure to obtain specified components.

Notice is also given that if equipment that is still under warranty is modified in any way or used or connected with home-built equipment then that warranty may be void.

© 1989 BERNARD BABANI (publishing) LTD

First Published — August 1989

British Library Cataloguing in Publication Data
Penfold, J. W.
    A concise introduction to GEM
    1. Microcomputer systems. Operating systems: GEM
    I. Title
    005.4'469

ISBN 0 85934 175 5

Typeset direct from disk by EMSET, London NW10
Printed and Bound in Great Britain by Cox & Wyman Ltd, Reading

CONTENTS

Preface

Though GEM is designed to be easy to use, with anything in computing a little help at first is welcome. There will also be times when even experienced users find that although they know something can be done, they cannot quite remember how to do it. These are the twin purposes of this book. In the first instance it is an introduction to the GEM environment for complete beginners, in the second it gives clear instructions for the various tasks which GEM can perform. To avoid forward and backward references, these sections have been made complete in themselves, which means that some information has been repeated. Though I thought at one time that front ends like GEM might only have a short life, this is clearly not the case. They are here to stay. They can make some of the boring parts of computing, if not exactly fun, at least pleasant occupations. I hope you will find it so.

J. W. Penfold.

PLEASE NOTE:

In this book, the names of menus which appear in the GEM menu bar are given in all-capital letters, e.g. FILE, to help them stand out in the text. On screen, the names are in upper and lower case. Options on menus are enclosed in inverted commas, e.g. "Open".

TRADEMARKS:

GEM, GEM Desktop, GEM Paint, GEM Draw and GEM Write are registered trademarks of Digital Research Inc.

1st Word Plus and Timeworks Desktop Publisher are registered trademarks of GST Holdings Ltd.

Amstrad is a registered trademark of Amstrad Consumer Electronics PLC.

IBM and PC/DOS are registered trademarks of the IBM corporation.

Atari is a registered trademark of Atari Corporation.

Apple, Apple Macintosh and Apple Lisa are registered trademarks of Apple Corporation.

BASIC 2 is a trademark of Locomotive Software Ltd.

MS/DOS is a trademark of Microsoft Corporation.

Chapter 1

WHAT IS GEM?

GEM is a system for making computers easier to use, or "user friendly", if you don't object to jargon. The idea of friendly computers seems to have started in the laboratories of the Xerox Corporation, best known for photocopiers, in Palo Alto, California. They designed a system which used pictorial representations of files rather than just a list of file names on a screen, and an on-screen "pointer" moved by a "mouse" to select files. These ideas were never used in a commercial product by Xerox, however.

Next on the scene was Apple Computers, with their Lisa computer. This had a graphically-based operating system, with mouse and pointer, and was a magnificent computer, but never sold in great numbers. However, Apple kept with it and next produced the now famous Macintosh (actually named after a variety of apple popular in the United States) which was (and is) a commercial success. The popularity of the Macintosh gave rise to a number of products designed to add a graphical file management system to other computers, and GEM is one of these.

GEM can be bought as a product and added to computers which have an operating system suitable for it, or it can be supplied with the computer when purchased. In the latter case, it may be used as an option to control the operating system, with a conventional command line interpreter also available, or it may be integrated into the system so that control is only possible via GEM.

GEM is not itself an operating system. As it is available for several different operating systems, it follows that the facilities offered by GEM will differ somewhat depending on what the underlying O.S. provides. GEM cannot add facilities to an O.S., but in some cases it can appear to do so by allowing what would be a series of system commands to be given in a single action. GEM does not necessarily give access to all the features provided by an operating system.

To understand what GEM is and does, it is helpful to know about the relationship of hardware, software and operating system. On its own, the computer hardware (CPU, memory,

1

disk drives, keyboard, screen etc.) can do very little. To do useful work, it needs to have a program loaded and running.

If every programmer who wanted to write an application (wordprocessor, database, spreadsheet etc.) had first to write routines to read a character from the keyboard, write data to disk and so on, it would make programming very tedious, so most computers come complete with an operating system, consisting of a set of general-purpose routines to do these tasks. The operating system also acts as an intermediary between hardware and software, and can allow the same program to be used on computers with slightly different hardware.

The operating system is also used directly by the user for such tasks as loading and running programs, and copying disks, as well as some more complex tasks. It is here that problems can arise. The commands which must be typed into the operating system (strictly, into the command line interpreter or CLI), can be complex and quite long, and not at all easy to remember. It is here that the graphic representations of GEM are a great help.

GEM also provides a set of graphics facilities which can be used by programs written to take advantage of them (conventionally termed GEM applications). In these cases, GEM sits between the application and the operating system. Thus, applications can work through the operating system only (in this book these will be referred to as non-GEM applications), or via GEM **and** the operating system. (In fact, it is also possible for applications to access the hardware direct, and this is done in some cases of animated games with fast action, but these will not directly concern us in this book.)

The Gem Desktop.
The part of GEM from which you select programs to be run, and perform copying operations etc. is called the GEM Desktop. When you buy a computer which is supplied with GEM it is the Desktop which is included with it (though you may also get one or two "bundled" GEM applications). You cannot normally buy GEM Desktop as a program for computers not supplied with GEM, but when you buy a GEM application, the Desktop will be supplied with it. Figure 1 shows a typical Desktop display.

GEM is often called a WIMP environment. This acronym

stands for Windows Icons Mouse Pointer. To take these one at a time:-

WINDOWS are areas of the screen. You can have more than one window on the screen, occupying separate areas or overlapping. If the windows overlap, one will be on top of the other(s), hiding all or part of the contents of those underneath. Windows can be added to the display by opening them, or removed by closing them, and in some cases can be moved around the screen (using the mouse) and changed in size.

Each window can contain display material, the screen's **contents,** and the area which the contents occupies can be larger than the display area of the window, so that only part of the contents is visible. In such cases, the contents can be scrolled within the window (vertically, horizontally, or both, as appropriate) to enable all the contents to be seen. It may be possible to increase the size of the window to display all the contents at once, but some windows are fixed in size.

In some versions of GEM, there are text windows and graphics windows. Text windows can display text only, in a single font only (i.e. text style and size is fixed). Graphics windows can display both text, in a variety of fonts, and also graphics (lines, shapes, fill patterns etc.). Other versions of GEM have only graphics windows. Where text windows are available, they use up less memory space (substantially so) for a given display area.

ICONS are the pictorial representations of files, etc. GEM has several types of icon. These include representations of the disk drives, folders, and various types of file. Early versions also have a trash can icon for deleting files, but this was removed following a legal dispute with Apple. Several of the other icon types have also been changed in design since the earliest versions.

In the early versions, the disk drives were represented as filing cabinet drawers. In current versions they are represented as pictograms of a floppy or hard disk, as appropriate. Where appropriate, you may also have a different icon representing a RAM disk, that is, an area of memory used as a pseudo-disk drive.

The folder icon is a pictogram of a card folder as used in filing cabinets to hold documents. Folders represent the operating system directories, and can hold files, or other folders.

Folder and Disk drive icons can be seen in Figure 1.

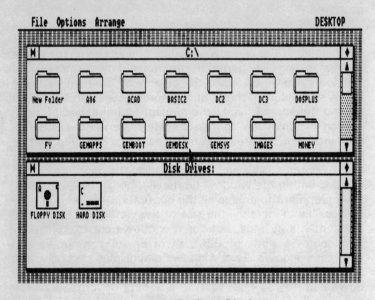

Fig 1. GEM Desktop Display

File icons can take several forms. Files which are executable programs are shown as rectangles with a bold line at the top. In the first version of GEM (as still used on the Atari ST series), all program icons are the same, but in Version 2 onward they can have additional pictorial information, for example a picture of a typewriter for a word processor or a hammer for a "toolkit" program.

Data files are shown as a sheet of paper with one corner folded up, and again there may be additional pictorial information in the icons for Version 2 onward. The icon for word processor documents has dotted lines on it, looking like paragraphs on a page, for example (see Figure 2).

The MOUSE is a device with buttons on top and a ball underneath, which is pushed around on a clear area of the desk. As the mouse is moved on the desk surface, its movements are echoed by movements of the pointer on the screen. The buttons are used to indicate when you want to take some action. Normally GEM uses a two-button mouse, but three-button types can also be used.

The mouse is used to select items on the screen by moving the pointer over the item (such as an icon) and pressing the left- most button. This is referred to as "clicking on" that item. In the case of icons, they are "highlighted" (by becoming bolder or being displayed in reverse video, depending on the computer) to indicate that they have been selected. Figure 2 shows some highlighted file icons. If you click on an icon, any icons already selected are de-selected.

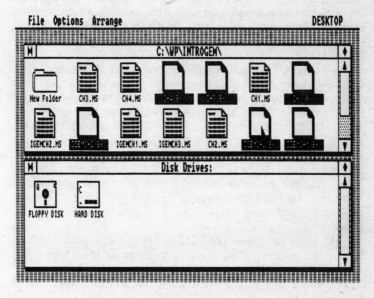

Fig   2. Highlighted File Icons

Programs can be run simply by moving the pointer to the icon for the program and clicking the left mouse button twice in quick succession. This is called "double clicking". With GEM applications, and some other programs, it is also possible to run the program by double-clicking on a data file generated by or appropriate to that program. The program will run and the data file will be loaded automatically for further work (there are various limitations on this).

When you want to select more than one icon, for example to copy multiple files, this can be done by "shift-clicking".

In most cases, this is done by clicking on icons with the left button, whilst holding down the right button. In some cases, however, you may have to use the shift key on the keyboard instead of the right button, and in the case of three-button mice, it may be the centre button, rather than the right-most which must be used. (The latest version of GEM, GEM/3, always uses the shift key on the keyboard.)

The remaining mouse action is dragging. This is performed by clicking on an icon, then holding down the left button and moving the pointer with the mouse. An outline of the icon will move with the pointer, and when the button is released the icon will jump to the new position. Dragging can be used just to move icons, but it is more commonly used in copying operations.

The POINTER is visible on the screen most of the time while GEM is running. It usually takes the form of an arrow. At times when the computer is "busy" the pointer will appear as an hourglass (or a "busy bee" on early versions). When this happens, the pointer is inactive (i.e. the mouse will not move it), so this could be thought of as the GEM equivalent of a "Please Wait" message. During copying operations, the pointer becomes a hand, used to "drag" the items to be copied.

The pointer may also take different forms in applications programs, for example as a brush, pencil or spray can in paint programs, and may appear as a floppy disk during disk operations.

GEM provides other facilities for those operations which cannot be performed solely with the use of the mouse and icons. These facilities are menus, dialogue boxes, and alert boxes. Many operations involve the use of more than one of these.

Menus allow a simple choice from a list of possible actions. When GEM is running, the names of all available menus appear in a line at the top of the screen. The actual menus available will differ depending on what GEM application is running. When the pointer is moved into this line near a menu name, that menu will pop down. In GEM/3 you can opt to have the menus only come down if you click the mouse button. This can be useful with graphics programs and the like, as it avoids accidentally bringing a menu down when using the mouse near the top of the screen. Items from that menu can then be selected with the mouse. After selection, the menu will pop back up.

On some menus, some items will appear in pale lettering, others in dark lettering. In such cases, the dark items are the only ones currently applicable and are the only ones which can be selected at that time.

If you accidentally pop down a menu which you do not want, it can be cleared from the display by clicking the mouse with the pointer anywhere on the screen outside the menu. A menu will also disappear if you move the pointer to the name of any other menu, being replaced by the new menu.

Dialogue boxes are used mostly when some information must be typed in to the computer, for example, a file name if you want to create a new folder. They appear in the middle of the screen. They also are used when you request information about a file from the FILES menu, and when you want to copy or delete files. In the latter case, the alert box will indicate how many files are to be copied or deleted, and ask you to confirm that you wish to proceed. It will then indicate a "count down" as the files are dealt with. Dialogue boxes normally have two "buttons", small rectangles within the box, with "OK" and "Cancel" in them. Clicking on "OK" confirms that you want to proceed. Clicking on "Cancel" cancels the whole operation. However, in some cases, alert boxes may just have the "OK" button, or may have additional or different buttons, relevant to the operation. In some cases where multiple operations are concerned, the "Cancel" button may only abort the current part of the operation.

Alert boxes are the GEM form of error messages. They appear to tell you if you have made a mistake or if GEM has been asked to do something it cannot do, for example, delete a read-only file, or if a problem has occurred with the system, such as a failure to read a file. Where a failure has occurred, the Alert box will normally have "Retry" and "Cancel" buttons in it. In other cases, there may just be an "OK" button, enabling you to acknowledge the error and regain control of the system.

Controlling GEM Windows.
Each GEM window has a border, and in the border are features which are used to control the window, and which also indicate (by their presence or absence) what actions are possible with that window.

In the bottom right corner of the window there is a symbol

7

of a square with an arrow coming from it. If you drag with the pointer on this symbol, the window can be increased or reduced in size, horizontally, vertically, or both simultaneously. When you make the screen larger, if there are more contents to the window than could be displayed in its original size, the extra contents will be displayed in the new area. If not, the new area will be blank. GEM cannot scale up the contents to fill the new area. When you reduce the size of a window, you do not lose any of the contents of the part now removed from the display. If this symbol is absent, the window is of fixed size.

The window can be moved around on the display by dragging with the pointer anywhere in the top border of the screen, called the title border because the title of the window or program will appear in it. During the moving operation, a dotted outline of the screen will move, the actual window and contents only moving when the new position is settled. You cannot drag a window so that any part of it moves out of the screen area.

In the top right corner of the screen is a diamond shape. This is called the full-screen toggle. Clicking with the pointer on this symbol will increase the window to full screen size. Clicking on it again will reduce the window back to the size it was before. Again, this symbol will be absent in a fixed-size screen.

If the bottom and right-hand borders are plain, all the contents of the window can be displayed within the current window size. If the borders are shaded, with clear bars (called ''sliders'') in them, there is more contents than can be displayed, and the slider represents the part of the contents which can be displayed, and its position within the total contents. In Figures 1 and 2, the top windows have sliders and the bottom windows do not. As you add to the contents, the bar area will get smaller.

When there is more contents than can be displayed, the window can be scrolled. There are two ways of doing this. Firstly, at the ends of the bottom and right borders there are arrowhead symbols. If you click with the mouse pointer on these, the screen will scroll by the smallest sensible increment for the nature of the display. If text, it will be one line of text, if icons, it will be one row of icons, and if a graphics display, it will be one pixel.

For faster scrolling of large distances, you can drag with the pointer anywhere within the slider. An outline of the slider will move, and the actual bar will move when you release the mouse button, and at this time the screen will scroll to the selected part of the display.

Finally, in the top left corner is a bow-tie symbol. If you click with the pointer on this, you will close the window, returning the display to what it was before the window was opened.

Customising the Desktop Display.

When GEM desktop starts normally the initial display will show icons representing the disk drive(s), hard or floppy, which are fitted to the machine. It is possible to alter this display so that, for instance, the display goes directly into a display of the root directory of the hard disk (if fitted). There are also other aspects of the desktop which can be altered to suit personal needs or preferences.

The things which can be changed include the size and position of the desktop windows, whether file information is displayed as icons or as text, whether sound effects are on or off (on appropriate machines), and how the mouse and keyboard (in some cases) respond. There may also be features which are machine-specific, such as control of colour palette.

The way in which changes are made differ somewhat on different versions of GEM. On early versions there is a "Control Panel" display, selected from the DESK menu. Some changes are made using this, and some using the "Set Preferences" option on the OPTIONS menu. Later versions of GEM do not have a DESK menu, and all the changes are on the "Set Preferences" display. Figure 3 shows the GEM 2 OPTIONS menu.

Most of the changes which can be made are self-explanatory and largely a mater of personal preference, but there are some points worth making. (A full description of all menus and options is given in Chapter 2.)

Most people chose the option to display files as text in order to display more file names on the screen at a time. If you choose to display files as text rather than as icons, as well as the name of the file, additional information will be displayed, such as the size of file, date it was last accessed, date it was created, etc. The exact information and the form in which it is displayed will depend on the underlying operating system.

9

If your operating system provides a lot of such information, it is by no means certain that more files will be displayed.

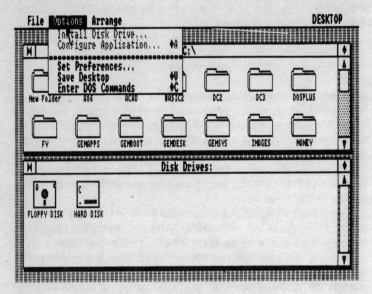

Fig 3. The GEM 2 Option Menu

It is quite common for newcomers to GEM to find that they cannot double-click the mouse fast enough when selecting programs to run from the desktop. There is an option, therefore, to slow down the double-click response. When you have gained some experience, however, you are quite likely to want to speed up the response again.

Similarly, on those systems which allow it, the keyboard response option allows you to select how long a key must be held down before it auto-repeats, and how fast it repeats when held down beyond this period. Making the auto-repeat delay too short can result in unwanted repeat characters, whereas if the period is too long, it is quicker just to strike the key twice. Trained touch typists will probably never want to use the auto-repeat anyway, and may prefer a longer delay.

Two other options determine whether you are asked to con-firm (by means of a dialogue box) file copying and deleting options when you have selected these by selecting icons. On the one hand, this is a useful safety precaution against making mistakes, on the other it takes up time. Many users compromise by choosing "yes" to the "Confirm Deletes" preference and "no" to "Confirm Copies". Copying a file, after all, does not destroy it.

It is normal to have two windows on the desktop displaying file icons, and these can be set up to show whatever directories you wish. If you have two disk drives, you may want to use the two windows for a display of each drive. Note that if you set the desktop to display a directory of a floppy disk, there must be a disk in the drive, or GEM will stop with an Alert box until one is inserted. You will not be able to proceed further without inserting a disk.

On the other hand, you may prefer to have a display of the root directory of one drive in one window, and a display of the directory for your most-used program in the other (particularly useful if you have a hard disk).

In version 1 of GEM, you may also alter the size and shape of the windows. It may be useful to have one bigger than the other, and if you prefer to display files as text, you may prefer to have two vertical windows side by side rather than the usual default of one above the other. In version 2 onward, the Desktop windows can only be toggled between half-screen (horizontal) and full- screen size.

Once you have set up the desktop the way you want it, you record the changes for future use with the "Save Desktop" option on the OPTIONS menu. This creates a special file on the disk with the Desktop programs, which is used whenever GEM is run in future. If you run GEM from floppy disks, and you have the Desktop on more than one, you must save your options on to all the disks from which you may run the desktop. It is, of course, perfectly possible to have different start-up options on different disks if this is helpful to you.

Chapter 2

DESKTOP MENUS AND ACCESSORIES

This chapter describes the menus available on the GEM desktop, and the options available on each menu. The arrangement of options varies somewhat depending on which version of GEM you are using. The menu differences between versions are described first, followed by a description of each option. Some options are not available on some versions. You may find machine- specific options on your Desktop which are not described here.

Version 1 GEM (as on Atari ST computers).
The menus are:
DESK FILE VIEW OPTIONS

The options for each menu are:-

DESK:

Desktop Info
VT52 Emulator
Control Panel
Set RS232 Config.
Install Printer

These options are machine-specific and will not be described, except to say that some of the options available from the Preferences menu on other versions are on the "Control Panel" here. The Install Printer option allows the computer to be set up to use a limited range of daisywheel and dot-matrix printers.

FILE:

Open ˙
Show Info
New Folder
Close
Close Window
Format

The "Show Info" is the same as "Info/Rename" on later versions. "New Folder" duplicates the effect of clicking on the

13

new folder icon. "Close Window" duplicates the effect of clicking on the bow-tie symbol. Both these have been deleted in later versions.

VIEW:

Show as Icons
Show as Text
Sort by Name
Sort by Date
Sort by Type
Sort by Size

This is the ARRANGE menu on later versions.

OPTIONS:

Install Disk Drive
Install Application
Set Preferences
Save Desktop
Print Screen

This is essentially the same as later versions, except that some of the things found under "Set Preferences" on later versions are on the "Control Panel" on the DESK menu (on the Atari at least).

The "Print Screen" option does a screen-dump to printer, provided a suitable dot-matrix printer has been installed. This option may be absent on some machines.

Version 2 GEM (as on Amstrad computers and many others) The menus are:-
FILE OPTIONS ARRANGE DESKTOP
The options for each menu are:-

FILE:

Open
Info/Rename
Delete
Format
To Output
Exit to DOS

"To Output" may be absent on some machines. Figure 4 shows the FILE menu on an Amstrad PC1512, running GEM 2.

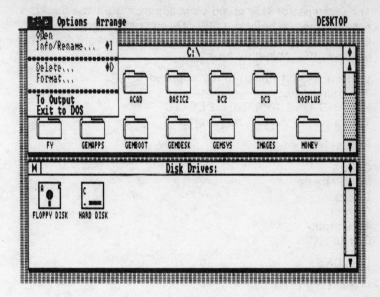

Fig 4. The Gem File Menu

OPTIONS:

Install Disk Drive
Configure Application
Set Preferences
Save Desktop
Enter DOS Commands

ARRANGE:

Show as Text (as Icons)
Sort by Name
Sort by Type
Sort by Size
Sort by Date

DESKTOP:

Desktop Info.
(Accessories as installed)

15

The contents of this menu vary depending on the Desktop accessories you have installed. They may include Calculator, Clock, Snapshot, Print Spooler. The Accessories are described at the end of this chapter.

Version 3 GEM (as currently supplied)
The menus are:-
FILE OPTIONS ARRANGE DESKTOP
The options for each menu are:-

FILE:

Open
Info/Rename
Delete
Format
To Output
Exit to DOS

OPTIONS:

Install Disk Drive
Configure Application
Set Preferences
Save Desktop
Enter DOS Commands

ARRANGE:

Show as Text (as Icons)
Sort by Name
Sort by Type
Sort by Size
Sort by Date

DESKTOP

Desktop info.
Print spooler
(Accessories as installed)

Accessories under GEM 3 are as for GEM 2, except that the Snapshot accessory seems to have been abandoned.

The Options.
Each of the options will now be described in alphabetical order. Where the option is too complex for a full discourse here, a

reference will be given to the chapter where it is fully described.

Configure Application. This is used to tell GEM about an application program, so that it can be run from the Desktop successfully. It is fully described in Chapter 4.

Delete. After an icon has been selected, this option can be used to delete whatever the icon represents, either a disk, folder or file. Multiple selections may also be deleted. However, read- only files cannot be deleted. Use with care, as deleted material cannot be recovered. Fully described in Chapter 4.

Enter DOS Commands. Allows you to temporarily enter the DOS environment, perhaps to enter commands not directly available from GEM. Much of GEM remains in memory, so if you try to run a large application program from here, it may not have enough memory space. When you have finished with DOS commands, you can return to GEM by entering EXIT at the DOS prompt.

Exit to DOS. This allows you to leave GEM permanently and enter the DOS environment. All of GEM is cleared from memory. To re-enter the GEM environment you must run GEM again as an application.

Format. This option allows you to format a floppy or hard disk. Formatting prepares the disk to receive data. Disks cannot be used until they are formatted. Formatting should be used with care, especially on hard disks, as it destroys any and all information currently on the disk.

Info/Rename. This option displays information about a disk, folder or file. An appropriate icon must be highlighted before this option can be selected. The information displayed depends on the object. In the case of disks (hard and floppy), you will see the disk identifying letter, the label (if any), the number of folders, the number of items (files), the bytes used and the bytes available. For folders you will see the name, the date created, the number of folders within, the number of items (files), and the bytes used. For files you will see the name, the size in bytes, the date last modified, and the attributes (i.e read-only, read/write). The information displayed may differ slightly depending on the underlying operating system. Figure 5 shows the information display for a hard disk.

Install Disk Drive. This option allows you to tell GEM about

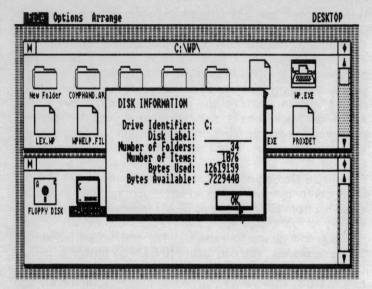

Fig 5. Hard Disk Information Display

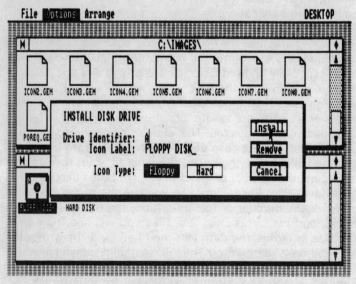

Fig 6. Install Disk Drive Dialogue Box

the disk drives - hard and floppy - attached to your machine. You can set and change the drive identifier. You should not have much need to use this option unless you add an extra drive to your machine. Drives attached to the machine will be automatically installed in GEM when GEM is installed in the machine. Figure 6 shows the dialogue box to install a disk drive.

Install Application. This is the same as Configure Application and is described in Chapter 4.

Open. After highlighting an icon, you can select this option as an alternative to double-clicking. This is useful if you find the double-click technique difficult, but using this option has no advantages or additional uses.

Set Preferences. In versions 2 and 3 of GEM, this option allows you to choose whether or not you want to confirm file delete and copy operations, the speed at which you must double-click the mouse, and whether or not you want sound effects. Version 3 allows you to set whether or not to confirm file over-

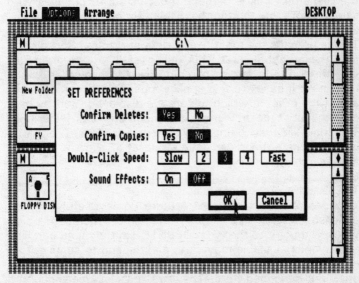

Fig 7. GEM 2 Set Preferences Dialogue Box

writes. On some version 1 installations, some of these preferences may be set elsewhere, for example on the Atari STs, some are on the Control Panel accessed from the DESK menu. See Figure 7.

Show as Text/as Icons. This allows you to choose how you want your files and folders, etc. to be displayed in the Desktop windows. In version 1 GEM, the two options are displayed on two lines, and a tick appears next to the one currently selected. On version 2 onward, there is just one line, and the option displayed changes. It shows "Display as Text" when icons are selected, and "Display as Icons" when text is selected, and changes from one to the other in a toggle action. Generally, displaying as text shows more information about the files, and may allow more to be displayed in a window at once, but it is generally easier to tell the difference between files and folders, and between data and program files, when icons are selected.

Sort by Name/Type/Size/Date. This option allows the order in which the files etc. are displayed in the window. Sort by name puts the files in alphabetical order of the first part of the filename. This is perhaps most useful to put files with similar name together on the display for copying operations. Sort by type puts the folders ahead of program and data files. This is perhaps the most useful default display. Sort by size puts the largest file first. This will generally put program files (which tend to be larger than data files) first in order, which may make it easier to find applications. This option does not affect the order in which folders are displayed. Sort by date puts the most recently created or modified file or folder first. This makes it easy to find your current work files. Thoughtful use of these options can save a fair bit of window scrolling and searching.

The Desktop Accessories.
Versions 2 and 3 of GEM feature some useful Desktop accessories which are listed on the menu which pops down when you point to the word DESKTOP in the menu bar. The accessories available may vary, and depend to some extent on what you choose to install, but the most generally available ones are described here. They are the clock/calendar, the calculator, "Snapshot", and the print spooler. (NOTE. Version 1 GEM also has "accessories" on the DESK menu, but

these tend to be machine-specific features.)

The accessories are generally available from within GEM applications as well as from the Desktop itself. However, with very large applications (DTP programs, perhaps), there may not be enough room in memory, and the accessories may be removed. They cannot be accessed from non-GEM applications, even if these have been run from the Desktop.

Installing the Accessories.

Because the accessories take up a considerable amount of memory space, not every user will want to install them. It is only worth doing so if you intend using them. Depending on your version of GEM, some of the accessories may be installed by default. Others may be supplied, but not installed. To install them, you must find the appropriate file, usually in the folders GEMBOOT or GEMSYS, and rename it with the extension ACC, using the Info/Rename option on the FILES menu. It will be supplied either without an extension, or with the extension ACX or similar. Once renamed, the accessory will become usable the next time you reboot GEM.

If you want to de-install an accessory to leave more RAM free, this can be done by the reverse action, changing the filename extension to something other than ACC. The accessory will remain available for the current session, but will not load the next time you re-boot GEM.

Note that re-booting in these instances includes returning to the desktop from an application (GEM or non-GEM) which needs full memory, but not returning from an application which allows the Desktop to remain in memory.

The Clock/Calendar.

The GEM clock is used to set and display the current time and date. Once set, it will keep reasonable time for as long as the computer is switched on. If your machine has a battery-backed real-time clock, this will be set when you set the GEM clock and thereafter, when GEM is booted, the GEM clock will be set automatically from the system clock. The GEM clock can be displayed at all times on the screen, with the Desktop and within applications, provided there is room in memory for it. It is shown in Figure 8.

To display the clock, select "Clock" from the DESKTOP menu. It will appear, displayed in its own window. To the left

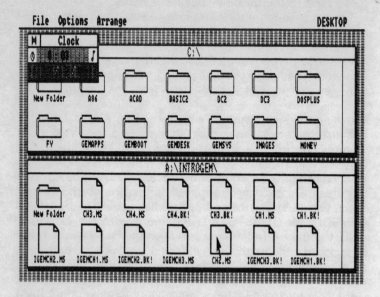

File Options Arrange   DESKTOP

Fig 8. The Clock Accessory

of the time display you will see a symbol. When the clock is
displaying the current time, this will be a clockface. If it is a
bell, the clock is displaying the set time for the alarm. To
change from one to the other, click on the symbol. The time
is always displayed in 24-hour form in GEM 2, but 12-hour
form can be selected in GEM/3. The current date is always
displayed. In UK supplied machines it will normally be in the
order dd/mm/yy, but on machines supplied in some other
countries it may be in another order, such as mm/dd/yy as
commonly used in the USA. GEM/3 allows the date format
to be switched between these two (as part of ''Set
preferences'').

   To set the time, you click on the appropriate part and enter
the new value. To set the hours, move the pointer anywhere
on the hours figures, and click once. You can then type in the
new value, but you must always enter two digits (e.g. 01,
08, 14, 23). Only valid values (00 to 24) will be accepted.
The hour is set when you type the second digit and no further action is necessary. The minutes are set in the same way

22

by clicking anywhere on the minutes figures, but this time, of course, the valid range is from 00 to 59. Again, you must type two digits and the minutes are set when you type the second digit. The clock cannot set or display seconds.

The date is set in much the same fashion. You click on the appropriate part, and enter two digits, the setting being made when you enter the second.

The clock is used to date- and time-stamp files as well as being for your convenience, so if you do not have a battery-backed clock, you should set it each time you use the computer.

The clock also has an alarm facility. This is set by clicking on the symbol to the left of the time display to change it to a bell (if necessary). The method of setting the alarm time is the same as for setting the real time. The alarm time setting can be checked at any time by clicking on the clockface symbol. Click on the bell to switch back to a real-time display. You will also see a musical note symbol to the right of the time display. If this is black, the alarm is set to go off. If it is grey (or red on some colour screens), the alarm will not sound. Click on this symbol to change from one to the other.

The alarm will sound at the time set provided the computer is not switched off. The alarm setting will also be lost if you select "Quit" or "Exit to DOS" from the FILES menu, or if you run an application which needs full memory, but not if you select "Enter DOS Commands" from the OPTIONS menu.

The clock/calendar may be left on display permanently. If it becomes partly hidden behind other windows, it may be brought to the top again by clicking on any part of it which remains visible. When no longer needed, it can be removed from the display by clicking on the bow-tie symbol.

The Calculator.
The GEM calculator has the features of a typical pocket calculator, which the screen display very much resembles, as shown in Figure 9. When you select "Calculator" from the DESKTOP menu, the calculator appears in the middle of the screen.

You can enter numbers into the calculator either by clicking on the buttons with the mouse, or by using the numeral keys on the keyboard. If your computer has a separate numeric keypad, you will usually have to use these, rather than the

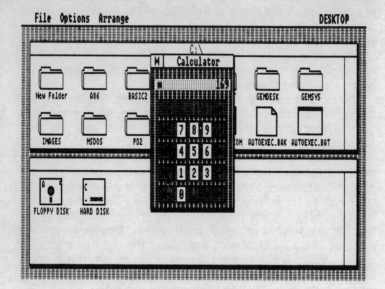

Fig 9. The Calculator Accessory

keys above the letter keys. You may also have to press the
"Num Lock" key.

You can also use the keyboard to enter " + " and " − ". As
in computer languages, the backslash "/" is used for division,
and the star "*" for multiplication. "MR" can be entered by
pressing "m" followed by "r", and other keys with two letters can be entered in similar fashion. However, the sign
change key, which has " +/− " on it, is entered from the
keyboard with the "\" key.

The calculator follows operator precedence in chain calcula-
tions. This means that multiplication and division will be done
before addition and subtraction. (A "chain calculation" is one
where you enter several operations before pressing the " = "
key.)

The percentage function is of the type which will
immediately display a simple percentage. For example, if you
enter
40 + 12.5%
the calculator will display
5

24

If you then press the "=" key, the percentage will be added in, and the display will show
45

The calculator has a single memory. When the memory is in use an "m" will appear to the left of the display. If this is present when the calculator is first selected, the memory will hold 0.

The calculator need not be removed from the display when you have finished with it. To resume work in another window, click with the mouse anywhere in that window. The calculator may be brought back into use by clicking on any visible part of it. To remove it completely from the display, click on the bow-tie symbol.

Snapshot.

The Snapshot accessory is a method of capturing the whole or part of the screen display, and storing it in a file suitable for subsequent loading into GEM PAINT, or other programs which use .IMG files, or for directly printing using GEM OUT-PUT. Of course, many computers have screen dump facilities built into the operating system, but Snapshot allows only part of the screen to be captured, and also printing via GEM OUT-PUT allows some flexibility of final image size, which O.S. screen dumps do not.

Snapshot is found (as far as the author can determine) on version 2 GEM only. Version 2 GEM Snapshot will not work under version 3, so if you make frequent use of this accessory you should think twice about upgrading to version 3.

Snapshot is the largest program among the GEM accessories, and so should not be loaded if memory capacity is tight on your machine. It also needs a fair amount of disk space to save the images, and this can be a problem with floppy-disk based systems using low- density 360K drives.

As with the other accessories, Snapshot is only available from within GEM based programs. It cannot be used in conjunction with O.S. based programs, even if they are run from the GEM Desktop.

To use Snapshot, pop down the DESKTOP menu and select it. Your current program will be suspended and a picture of a camera will appear in the middle of the screen, as shown in Figure 10. To proceed with the screen capture, click with the pointer anywhere on the camera image. To cancel, click on the bow-tie symbol.

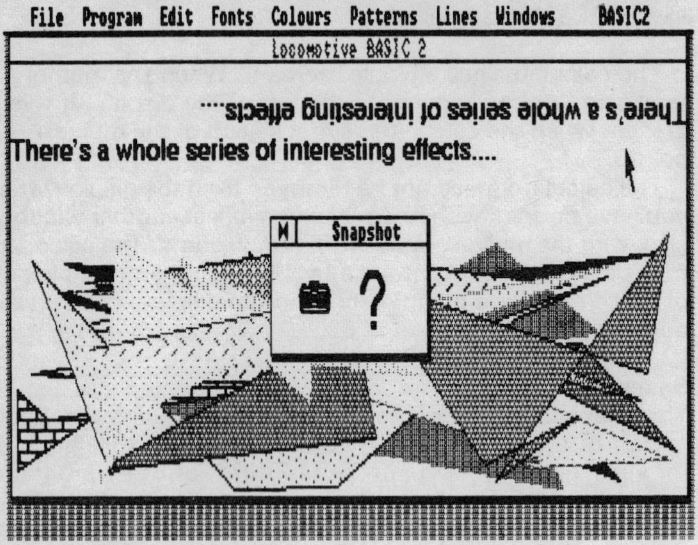
File Program Edit Fonts Colours Patterns Lines Windows BASIC2
Locomotive BASIC 2
There's a whole series of interesting effects....
There's a whole series of interesting effects....
Snapshot
?

Fig 10. The Snapshot Accessory

If you proceed, you must next enter the file name to be used for the stored picture. The filename must be given the extension .IMG (e.g. SCREEN1.IMG) as this extension is used by GEM PAINT and other programs to identify files of this type. When you press the return key after entering the filename, the screen image will be restored to what it was before Snapshot was selected.

You can now select the part of the screen image you want to capture. Move the pointer to the top left corner of the area with the mouse, and then hold down the left mouse button and drag the pointer to the lower right corner, then release the mouse button. The image area will be written to disk file, and your original program will then continue.

Chapter 3

FILE HANDLING WITH GEM

Files and Folders

The operating systems under which GEM runs use a hierarchical file structure. The point of this system is that, if you have a lot of files (and on a hard disk one can very rapidly get into the thousands), it can be very hard to find the one you want on the display. To keep things within reason, groups of files are stored together in the "folders". When you double click on a disk icon the display you see is called the "root directory", and may consist largely of folders.

When you double-click on a folder icon, the screen display will change to show the contents of the folder, which may be files, but may also contain further folders. You can again display the contents of these by double-clicking on the icon. You can continue like this as far as there are further folders.

To move back to a previous level in the file structure, it is necessary simply to click on the bow-tie symbol to close the window. When you do this the display returns to the previous level. The file structure is shown diagrammatically in Figure 11.

There may be a definite limit to how many levels you may have in the file structure (like 8 levels), or the limit may be so high that you will never reach it in practice (like 256 levels), or there may be no limit other than that imposed by disk space. Few people use more than three or four levels, however.

On a hard disk system, it is usual to place each application program (word processor, database, spreadsheet, accounts) in a separate folder. Within this folder, it can be useful to organise the data files generated by the program into several folders. With a word processor, for example, you may have a folder for personal correspondence, a folder for business correspondence, and one or more for other documents. If you generate a large amount of business correspondence, it would be better to have a separate folder for each client.

As well as keeping things tidy, intelligent use of folders can also simplify file naming. With letters, for instance, if you use a separate folder for each correspondent the filename for each letter can be based solely on date, and this will also make it

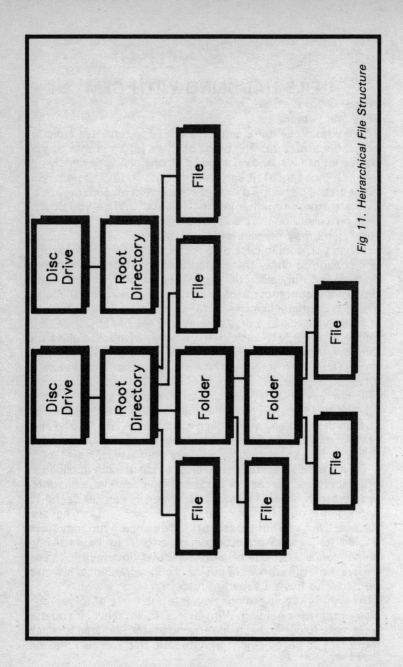

Fig 11. Heirarchical File Structure

easier to find a particular letter. Some programs, however, may restrict your use of folders, and require their files to be stored in a specific place.

On a system solely based on floppy discs, the use of folders is less important as each disk can hold much less data, and hence many fewer files, than a hard disk. You may, however, like to use folders to group data files just as on a hard disk, in effect treating each floppy disk as if it were a folder in a hard disk root directory. If you subsequently acquire a hard disk, it will then be a very easy matter to transfer the files onto it and have them in a suitably structured form.

You should try to keep your files in a suitably structured form right from the start. If you do not do this, and have to start organising them when you already have a lot of files on disk, you will find it a time-consuming and taxing operation, and there is also a risk of either wasting disk space by failing to delete old unwanted copies of files, or worse, of losing files you need to keep. However, the remainder of this chapter should tell you everything you need to know to do it.

Icons or Text
In this chapter, descriptions of operations assume the default of displaying disks, files and folders as icons. If you have chosen the option of displaying as text, the operations remain fundamentally the same, but you will place the mouse pointer anywhere on the text line rather than anywhere on the icon.

Copying an Entire Floppy Disk to Floppy Disk
The way in which this is done depends on whether you have one or two floppy disk drives. Before beginning disk copying you should, of course, make sure you have sufficient blank formatted disks for the copies you wish to make (though some copying methods can format a disk during the copying process).

1. Two Disk Drives. You must have a blank, formatted disk ready to receive the data. You should be at the GEM Desktop display, with the icons for both floppy disk drives displayed. Place the disk to be copied in one drive, and the blank, formatted disk in the other. Highlight the icon for the disk drive containing the disk to be copied, then hold down the left mouse button and drag to the icon for the drive containing the blank disk. Release the mouse button.

Unless you have suppressed the "confirm copies" option, you will see a GEM dialogue box which will tell you how many files/folders are to be copied. Click on the "OK" button to start the copying operation. You will see a "count down" as the files are copied. On early versions this appears graphically as two bars with shaded areas representing the files on the disks. As copying proceeds, the shaded area for the destination disk grows to match that for the source disk. On later versions, the count-down is exactly that.

2. Single Disk Drive. If you have a single disk drive (with or without a hard disk), but two **floppy** disk icons, labelled A and B, are shown on the desktop display, you can proceed as for a two-disk machine, by dragging the icon for drive A over to the icon for drive B. You will be periodically requested to swap disks as necessary.

The Author has experienced problems when copying disks in this way. You may find the number of disk swaps required to be excessive. You may also find that the messages to swap disks come direct from the operating system rather than through GEM, so that the Desktop screen display is corrupted. If you have either of these problems, try using the method described next. (In fact the Author found this more trouble than it was worth, and "uninstalled" logical drive B!)

If you have a single floppy drive and this is shown only as drive A on the desktop display, copying an entire disk cannot be done directly from the Desktop. It must be done by using a program which in most operating systems is called "Diskcopy". This will normally be found in the directory of the disk containing the operating system with the name of the operating system. Look for a folder called MSDOS or DOSPLUS or whatever your operating system is, and display its contents. Find the icon for this program and run it by double-clicking on it, or by highlighting it and selecting the "open" option from the FILE menu.

You will be presented with a dialogue box which will show the name of the application, and will have under that a line titled "Parameters". On this line will be a cursor, ready for you to type in information. You should enter:-

A: B:

Note that there is a space between the first colon and the B, and you may use upper or lower case letters. You will then be prompted to insert, in turn, the source and destination disks into the drive. The disks may need to be swapped a number of times, depending on how much free memory is available.

When the copying is complete, you will probably be offered the option of copying further disks. If you say no to this (by striking the "N" key on the keyboard), you will be returned to the GEM Desktop display.

When copying disks by any of the above routes, what you produce is an exact track-for-track and sector-for-sector "carbon copy" of the source disk. Any files on the destination disk will be lost. If you use a named disk for the copy, the name will be overwritten and the copy disk will bear the same name (if any) as the source disk. On most operating systems, Diskcopy (or the equivalent) can format while copying, so it may not be necessary to format disks before using them as destination disks.

3. Copying via Hard Disk. If you have a hard disk and a single floppy drive, and you find the use of Diskcopy troublesome, perhaps because of the number of disk swaps required, you can copy via a temporary folder on the hard disk. The procedure is as follows.

Display the hard disk root directory and open a new folder by double-clicking on the new folder icon. Call this folder "Temp". Display the floppy disk icon in the other window, and drag it to the "Temp" folder. (You will get the usual dialogue window if you have not suppressed the "confirm copies" option.) When copying is complete, remove the source disk and insert the destination disk in the drive. Then drag the "Temp" icon to the floppy disk icon. When this copying is complete, delete the "Temp" folder, by dragging it to the trash can in early versions, or by highlighting it and selecting the "Delete" option from the FILES menu in later versions.

(If you have a RAM disk, you can also use this as a temporary storage area for floppy disk copying, provided the size of the RAM disk is sufficient to take all the files on the disk.)

Copying a disk in this way does not produce a "carbon copy" of the source disk, and any name given to the destination disk will be preserved. Files already on the destination disk will be preserved, so you should be sure there is sufficient free space on the destination disk for the files you want to copy onto it.

Bear in mind that some disks on which commercial software

is provided are copy-protected to prevent the production of "pirate" copies.

Copying an Entire Floppy Disk to Hard Disk.
Normally when you want to copy an entire disk onto a hard disk, you will want to put the contents into a folder. However, the files on the floppy disk may already be in a folder, or you may want to copy the files to the root directory for some reason. NOTE: The procedure for installing a new program is covered in Chapter 4.

1. Copying to the Root Directory. Display the hard disk and floppy disk icons in the same or separate windows. Put the disk to be copied in a floppy drive and then drag the icon for that drive to the hard disk icon. If you have not suppressed the "confirm copies" option you must click on "OK" when the dialogue box appears. If all or any files on the floppy disk are in folders, they will also be in those folders on the hard disk. Files in the root directory of the floppy disk will be in the hard disk root directory.

2. Copying to an Existing Folder. Display the icon for the folder to receive the disk files in one window and the icon for the floppy disk drive in the other. Place the source disk in the drive, then drag the drive icon to the folder icon. If you have not suppressed the "confirm copies" option you must click on 'OK" when the dialogue box appears. Files in the root directory of the disk will be placed directly in the folder. Any files in folders on the disk will remain in those folders within the destination folder. Be careful not to exceed the number of levels of folder allowed by your operating system.

3. Copying to a New Folder. Display the directory for the level at which you wish to create the new folder and either double-click on the "New Folder" icon, or highlight the icon and then select the "Open" option from the FILES menu. A dialogue box will appear in which you must enter the name for the new folder. With the new folder displayed in one window, you must display the icon for the floppy drive in the other window, then drag it to the new folder icon. If you have not suppressed the "confirm copies" option you must click on "OK" when the dialogue box appears. Any files in folders on the disk will remain in these folders within the destination folder. Be careful not to exceed the number of levels of folder allowed by your operating system.

Copying a Single File.

1. Copying to Another Folder. Display the icons for the file to be copied and the folder to which it is to be copied. These will probably have to be displayed in separate windows, but in some cases they may be displayed in the same window. Drag the file icon to the folder icon. If you have not suppressed the "confirm copies" option you must click on "OK" when the dialogue box appears.

2. Copying Within One Folder. Display the folder icon in one window and the contents of the folder (including the file to be copied) in the other window. Drag the file icon to the folder icon. If you are copying the file to the same level within the folder, there will be a name conflict as you cannot have two files with the same name in the same directory. The operation will be aborted.

3. Copying a File Disk-to-Disk with One Drive. If you have one floppy disk drive, but it is shown on the display as two drives, you can proceed as above and you will be prompted to change disks as required during the copying operation. If your single drive is shown only as a single drive, you will have to perform the operation by copying the file temporarily either to hard disk or to RAM disk, and then copy it out to the new disk.

Copying Multiple Files.

If you want to copy several files (or several folders) to the same destination, it is possible to do this in one operation (with certain limitations). In general, this is done by highlighting the icons of all the files to be copied, then dragging one of these icons to the destination icon. However, all the icons for the files to be copied must be displayed in the same window at one time. It is not possible to highlight some files and then scroll the window and highlight more. If the window is scrolled, any highlighted icons which move out of the window will be de-highlighted automatically.

Both methods described here can be used to copy groups of single files, or groups of folders, or any combination of the two.

1. Shift-Click Method. Display the icons of the files to be copied in one window and the icon of the destination folder or disk drive in the other window. (In some cases it may be that the files and the destination appear in the same window.)

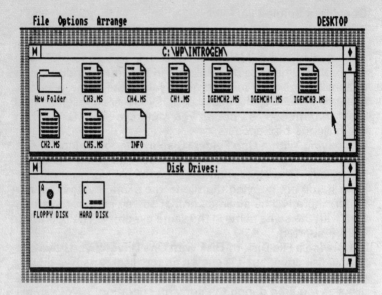

Fig 12. Boxing Files to be Copied

Place the pointer on the icon of the first file to be copied and, while holding down either the left mouse button or the shift key on the keyboard (as required by your system) click the right mouse button. The icon will be highlighted. Repeat this for each of the files to be copied. Keep the shift key or right mouse button depressed throughout this operation. When all the files to be copied have been highlighted, release both buttons (or key and button). Then, move the pointer to the icon of any of the files to be copied, press the right mouse button and keep it pressed, and drag that icon to the icon for the destination. If you have not suppressed the "confirm copies" option you must click on "OK" when the dialogue box appears. You will see a "count down" of the files as they are copied (the form of which depends on which version of GEM you are using).

2. Box Method. This method depends upon being able to display all the files to be copied in a contiguous area on the screen. The ability to do this depends to some extent on the use of the options available under the "Arrange" option on

34

the OPTIONS menu, which allows files to be grouped in order according to their filenames, dates of creation, or sizes. If this can be done, highlighting can be performed in one operation. Firstly, the icons for the files to be copied should all be displayed in one window, and the icon for the destination folder or disk drive in the other window. Move the pointer above and to the left of the top leftmost icon of the group of files to be copied. The pointer must **not** be actually on the icon. Press the left mouse button and keep it pressed. Move the pointer down and to the right. As it moves, a box of dotted lines will be drawn, with the starting point and the current position of the pointer as the top left and bottom right corners. This is shown in Figure 12. Move the pointer until this box encloses all the files to be copied, then release the mouse button. All the files within the box will be highlighted. Place the pointer on any of the highlighted icons, and drag it to the destination icon. If you have not suppressed the "confirm copies" option you must click on "OK" when the dialogue box appears.

With both of the above methods, should you change your mind about the copying operation, you can de-highlight the files by clicking with the pointer in any blank area of the screen.

Deleting a Disk, File, or Folder.
Note that files cannot be deleted if they have the read-only attribute set. Also, a folder cannot be deleted if it contains any files. Normally, when you delete a folder, GEM will first delete the files within the folder, and then the folder itself. If any of the files in the folder is read-only, the deletion operation will be aborted. To delete a read-only file, it must first be set to read-write. This is done by selecting the "Information/Rename" option from the FILE menu, and then clicking on "Read/Write" in the dialogue box.
1. "Trash Can" GEM Versions. Move the pointer to the icon for the disk, file or folder to be deleted, and drag it to the trash can icon. If you have not suppressed the "confirm deletions" option you must click on "OK" when the dialogue box appears. It is recommended that you do not suppress this option as once you have deleted a file it cannot be recovered.
2. Non-"Trash Can" Versions. Select the disk, file or folder icon by highlighting it. Pop down the FILES menu and select

the "Delete" option. If you have not suppressed the "confirm deletions" option you must click on "OK" when the dialogue box appears. It is recommended that you do not suppress this option as once you have deleted a file it cannot be recovered. Figure 13 shows a delete operation in progress.

Renaming a File.
There may be times when you want to change all or part of a file name. You may want to alter it to indicate that a file is no longer current, or because you gave it a silly name in the first place. To rename a file, first highlight its icon, then select the "Information/Rename" option from the FILE menu.

You can then enter the new name in the dialogue box. The old name will appear in the box with a cursor in the form of a vertical bar, and you can edit using the backspace(to delete), arrow and character keys. When entering a filename in a GEM dialogue box, illegal characters in filenames are not accepted, so if you type a character and it does not appear, this is the probable cause. Figure 14 shows the Information/rename box for a file.

Displaying a Directory of a Disk or Folder.
Firstly, display the icon for the disk or folder in one of the windows, then either double click on the icon, or highlight the icon and then select the "Open" option from the FILES menu. The display in the window will change to a display of the icons for the files/folders in the directory of the disk or folder. The title bar of the window will show the drive identifier for the disk and the name of the folder. The scroll bar at the right of the window will reveal whether all the files are displayed in the window, or whether there is an overflow. In the latter case, the window can be scrolled to allow all the icons to be inspected. It is also possible to increase the size of the window (in recent versions the desktop windows can only be toggled between half- screen and full-screen size, by clicking on the diamond symbol, top right corner).

If you have a display of the files on a floppy disk in a window and you change the disk in the drive, you can update the display by pressing the Escape key on the keyboard in most versions of GEM. If this does not work on your computer, you must close the window by clicking on the bow-tie symbol, and then click on the appropriate icon again to re-open it.

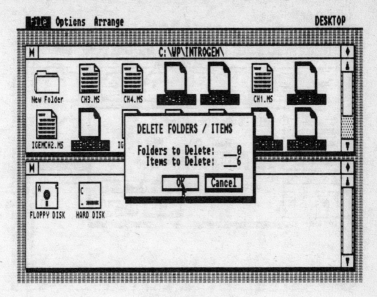

Fig 13. Deleting Files

To move back to the previous display, click on the bow-tie symbol (close window) in the top left corner of the window.

Information.
To display information about disk, file or folder, first display the appropriate icon in a window and highlight it by single-clicking. Then pop down the FILE menu and select the "Information/Rename" option. A dialogue box will appear. In the case of disks, it will show the drive identifier, name of disk (if any), number of folders, number of files, bytes used and bytes available. In the case of files it will show the name of the file, size in bytes, and the date and time when last modified, and also whether the file is read/write or read-only. In the case of folders it will show the folder name, number of folders within the folder, and number of files, also total size of all files in bytes. There may be slight differences to this with different operating systems and versions of GEM. Figure 15 shows the Information/rename box for a folder, and other examples will be found elsewhere in the book.

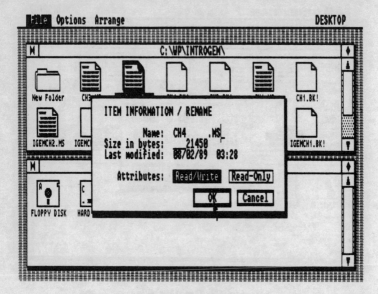

Fig 14. Information/Rename Box for a File

Renaming a Folder.

Folders cannot be renamed. If it is essential to do this, the only way is to create a folder with the new name, copy all the files from the existing folder into it, and then delete the old folder. Note that you must copy the files (individually or in groups). It is not sufficient to drag the icon for the existing folder to the icon for the new folder. If you do this, you will have the old folder within the new folder (though for some purposes this may be sufficient).

Security and Backup Copies.

When working on a large project, say a large drawing, a spreadsheet, or a book manuscript, it is normal to periodically save the work in progress to a disk file, so that in the event of a power cut or similar hiatus, only the (hopefully) small amount of work since the last save is lost. Most programs have a Save facility to do this, and in some cases a facility is included to automatically save the work in progress every

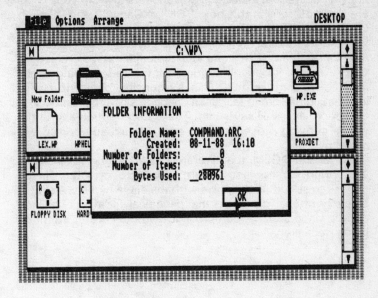

Fig 15. Information/Rename Box for a Folder

few minutes. The word processor used by the Author has such a facility.

It is also a good idea to make copies of the stored files at the end of every work session (and possibly during it) so that you have two copies, which can be stored in different places, as an insurance against one being corrupted. These are true backup files, not to be confused with previous versions of files which are saved by many operating systems with a BAK filename extension. As work progresses and you want to update your backup files, this will involve copying files on one disk to another disk where files with the same name already exist. The way in which GEM responds to file name conflicts varies from version to version, and may also depend to some extent on the underlying operating system.

On version 1 GEM installations particularly, it may not be possible to copy to a file of the same name at all. In these cases, the only possibility is to rename the files on the destination disk before copying.

On version 2 GEM, if a name conflict occurs during a

copying operation, a dialogue box appears to warn you. There are three buttons in this box, "OK", "Cancel" and "Stop". Clicking on "OK" will overwrite the original file with the new version. Depending on your operating system, the old version may be retained, with a changed filename extension (usually to BAK). The "Cancel" option allows the copying to be aborted **for that file only**. This is a sensible choice if the file in question has not in fact been changed since the last backup operation, as it will save time. The "Stop" option aborts the whole copying procedure, but any files already copied will remain.

On version 3 GEM, the "Preferences" dialogue box includes the option to suppress confirmation of overwrites. If you choose to suppress this, files with the same name will simply be overwritten. This means that periodical updating of backup copies, once started, can proceed without further attention being necessary.

Chapter 4

APPLICATIONS PROGRAMS

Applications are the programs you run to make your computer do useful work. They include wordprocessors, used to create letters and other documents, databases, used to organise, store and manipulate information, spreadsheets, used for financial planning and analysis, accounts programs, graphics programs and many others.

The term "applications" can also be used to include utility programs, like the Diskcopy program mentioned in Chapter 2. In fact, if you run a computer language on your machine to write programs, this language itself can be considered an application.

In the context of GEM, applications need to be considered in two broad categories. These are GEM applications, programs specifically written to use the graphics and other facilities provided by the GEM environment, and applications written without reference to GEM, using the operating system directly, which in this book are termed non-GEM applications. Both types of program can, however, be selected and run from the GEM desktop.

Installing GEM Applications.

When a new application is first purchased, it cannot normally be simply loaded and run as a game on a home computer can be. It will usually have to be set up to run on the particular combination of equipment to be used. It may, for instance, need to be told the type of display in use, the type of mouse, the type of printer, etc., and also how many disk drives the machine has and whether it is to run from floppy disks or a hard disk. On a hard disk especially, it may also be necessary to set up folders to take the program itself, and the files it generates. This process is termed installation.

For applications which are to use GEM, this procedure is often simpler than for non-GEM applications. GEM applications almost invariably come with a program called INSTALL.APP on the distribution disk(s) (the disk(s) on which the application is supplied), and installing the program consists of running

41

this program and typing in any information asked for. This program will set up any necessary folders, and ensure that the application can be run either by double-clicking on the program icon, or by double-clicking on the icon for a data file created by the program or appropriate to it.

If you are working from floppy disks, part of the installation process will probably be making working copies of the disks on which the software is supplied. These copies should always be used to run the program, keeping the distribution disks in a safe place in case the working copies should be damaged or corrupted.

If you are installing a program on a hard disk, you may have to run the Install program from the floppy disk drive, or you may have to copy all the files onto the hard disk and then run the Install program. Make sure you read the instructions carefully and don't jump to conclusions or rely on previous experience.

Running a GEM Application.
There are two ways of running a GEM application. Which you use depends largely on whether you wish to work on a data file which already exists, or whether you wish to start on a new file.

If you wish to work on an existing file, display the file icon in one of the desktop windows, and either double-click on it, or highlight it by single-clicking and select the ''Open'' option from the FILES menu. The application will run, and the file you have selected will be loaded ready for use. The only proviso to this is that there may be limitations on where the files are stored. Normally the program will save files to the folder where it expects to find them. If you have saved to a different folder, or copied files to a different folder, you may not be able to directly run the program by clicking on the file icons. This may also happen if you change the three-letter extension to the file name, as it is this which GEM uses to associate files with programs.

On some versions of GEM, it is possible to specify several different filename extensions for a particular program. To do this, you must select the ''Configure Application'' option from the OPTIONS menu. On the resulting Dialogue box you will see a line titled ''Document Type''. This will have the default extension next to it. If the line has further sections to take further extensions, you can enter these by pointing to the next section with the mouse and clicking, then typing in the required extension. When you have finished, click on the Install box. To make this change permanent, you must save the Desktop, bearing in mind that this will save any other changes you have made to GEM in the current session. You should make sure the Desktop display is as you want it at startup before saving.

If you cannot run the program by selecting a file, you must run it from the application icon, and open the required data file from within the program by selecting the "Open" option from the FILE menu. A list of files for the program will appear in a GEM Item Selector, and the one you want can be selected with the mouse. However, the list that appears initially will be for the folder where the program puts its files by default, so these will be the files from which you could run the program directly.

To find a file in another folder, you will need to change the folder name which appears at the top of the list of files. You do this by clicking with the pointer anywhere on the folder (or directory, as it may be called) name. A vertical bar cursor will appear and you can then edit the existing name or enter a new one. When you have done this, clicking on the "OK" button will display the list of files in the new directory.

To open a GEM application to create a new file, display the icon for the application program in one of the desktop windows, and either double-click on it, or highlight it by single clicking and then select the "Open" option from the FILE menu. The program will run without loading a data file, and the new file can be started.

GEM Features Within Applications.
The advantage of GEM applications is that they continue the WIMP environment of the Desktop. The pop-down menus are available, though the actual menus provided will depend on the application. You will always, however, have the FILE menu, and also the Desktop accessories available.

Within GEM applications, file selection is by means of dialogue boxes with lists of files, called Item Selectors. When the list is long, the window containing it will have scroll bars and you can scroll up and down the list to find the file you want. Selecting it is then a matter of either double-clicking

43

on it, or highlighting it by single-clicking and then clicking on the "OK" button. It is also possible to type in the name of the file you require. Within the dialogue box you will see the word "Selection" with a vertical bar cursor beside it, and you can type in the filename here, and then either press the Enter or Return key on the keyboard, or click on the "OK" button.

GEM applications can also make use of the GEM graphics facilities. These include the ability to display text in several fonts (different type styles and sizes), and to draw lines, circles, boxes (with square or rounded corners), and to fill shapes with a set of fill patterns. An advantage of GEM is that, as well as being displayed on the screen, these graphics can also, with some limitations, be sent to a printer, and with some machines, also to other output devices, such as a pen plotter or camera device. GEM 3 can also produce Postscript files, used for typesetting.

GEM also provides a consistency between applications. Programs running under GEM have a similar "look" and "feel'. The way in which things are done, for instance the loading and saving of files, is the same, as is the way windows are sized and scrolled, so the process of learning to use a new program to full effect is much reduced.

GEM also provides a standard for interchange within programs. This is not just the ability to save part of a spreadsheet in a form which can be used by a word processor, for instance (many non-GEM applications can do this), but the ability to exchange graphics. Pictures produced with GEM Paint, for instance, can be used within a GEM word processor or Desk Top Publishing (DTP) program, and screen images captured with the GEM Snapshot Desktop accessory can be worked on with GEM Paint. In fact, some illustrations in this book were produced in this way.

Leaving a GEM Application.
To leave a GEM application you should select the "Quit" option from the FILES menu. You should not leave a GEM application by simply switching off the computer or in any other way. If you do, some of your important data may not be correctly saved to disk. When you exit the program properly, you will be prompted if any file saving is necessary.

On quitting the program, you will return to the Desktop display as it was when you ran the application. If you are working from floppy disks, this may involve some disk swapping. If you do not intend using the computer further, after removing any floppy disks from the drive(s), it is safe at this point to switch off.

Installing a Non-GEM Application.
The process of installing a non-GEM application consists of two parts. Firstly, the application must be installed on the computer, secondly, if it is required to run the program from the GEM Desktop from a data file, it must be installed into GEM. However, not all non-GEM applications are capable of doing this. To be suitable for running in this way, the application must be of the type which can take parameters after the program name when running it from the DOS prompt. The program manual will tell you if this is possible. In particular, you must be able to specify a data file which is to be loaded on running.

Instructions for installing applications for your computer should be given in the program manual, probably in a section called "Getting Started". As with GEM applications, if you are working from floppy disks, part of the installation will probably involve making working copies. The requirements of different programs are, however, too varied for any generally applicable advice to be given here, except to follow the instructions carefully.

To be suitable for installation into GEM, the initial program, the one you call to start up, must have an extension of COM, EXE, APP, or BAT, but this will almost invariably be the case. To install the program into GEM, you should first run GEM Desktop. You should then display the icon for the application (the actual application file, not necessarily the initial program) in one of the Desktop windows, and highlight it by clicking. You should then select the "Install Application" option from the OPTIONS menu (this may be "Configure Application" in some versions). You will then see a dialogue box into which you must enter certain information about the program. This is shown in Figure 16.

Firstly, you will be asked for the filename extension used by the program. Most programs will give files a default extension. It is likely to be DOC for word processors, DAT or DBF for databases, FIG or WKS for spreadsheets, and IMG or DWG for graphics/CAD programs. The program manual should tell you. It is only the files with this extension that you will be able to use to run the program directly.

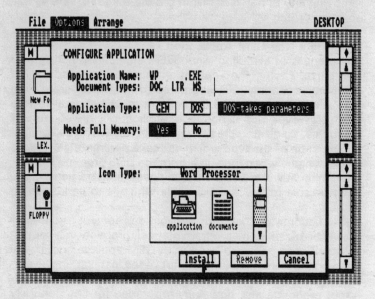

Fig 16. Configuring an Application

You can, in fact, have several different extensions for the one program on some versions of GEM. On these versions the line next to the "Document Type" will be broken. You can enter an extension of up to three letters on each section. To move to the next section of the line, point to it with the mouse and click. As an example, the Author's word processor is configured to accept the extensions DOC, LTR, or MS.

Next, you must set the application type, which can be GEM, DOS, or DOS-takes parameters. You should only select GEM for applications which are written to use the GEM features. If you select GEM for any other applications, they will not run. You should select DOS-takes parameters if you are sure that the application can take parameters as described above. If the application cannot take parameters, or you are not sure if it can, you should select DOS. You make the selection by moving the pointer to the appropriate box with the mouse and clicking.

DOS programs can only be run by clicking on the program icon. On some computers you may see the actual name of the operating system in the boxes instead of the generic term DOS. For example, on the Atari ST computers it is TOS. In the case of programs for the Ataris, you can usually tell what type they are by the extension to the filename. GEM programs are denoted by PRG, TOS programs by TOS, and TOS-takes parameters by TTP.

It is only GEM and DOS-takes parameters applications which can be run by clicking on an appropriate file icon. There may also be restrictions on where the data files are stored. This depends to some extent on the application, but in general it is necessary either for the files to be in the same folder as the program file, or in a specific folder within that folder. If the program can take a full file specification, including filename, directory and subdirectories, as a parameter then you should be able to put the files anywhere convenient to you. If the program can only take the filename as a parameter, then the files must be kept where the program expects to find them.

The second aspect of the problem is that GEM (or rather the operating system) must be able to find the application program when you click on a file icon. The ability of the operating system to do this varies from system to system. In some cases it may be essential for the application program to be in the same folder as the data file. In others the program can be anywhere, provided the operating system has been told where to look.

In the case of computers using the MS-DOS or PC-DOS operating systems, there is a command PATH to tell the O.S. where to look for files. When you open a program from a data file, these operating systems will first look for the program file in the current directory (the one where the data file is). If the program is not there, they will next look in the root directory of the current drive. If the program is not there either, the search will be performed according to the most recently executed PATH command (if one has been executed).

The PATH command can be thought of as a series of route instructions for the operating system to search in turn. Each set of instructions takes the form:

DRIVE ID:\DIRECTORY\SUBDIRECTORY\SUBDIRECTORY...

and within the PATH command each set is separated by a semicolon. The following are all examples of legal routes for use in a path command.

C:\	(Root directory)
C:\MSDOS	(One level)
C:\WP	(One level)
C:\CAD\PGF	(Two levels)

These can be put into one PATH command like this:

PATH C:\;C:\MSDOS;C:\WP;C:\CAD\PGF

Path commands always look confusing because of the preponderance of colons, semicolons and slashes, but remember that the semicolons are the separators between separate path routes.

When a path command has been set, the operating system will search for a file, taking each route in turn. Note that it is only the final directory in each route which is searched, also you can specify different drives in one PATH command if required.

Because the paths are searched in the order in which they are given in the command, it is best to put the path to the program you use most early in the list, to save time, but it should not be put ahead of the root directory or the DOS system files (C:\ and C:\MSDOS in the example above).

Each time you add an application program to your computer (especially if you have a hard disk) it is a good idea to add a path to the folder containing the program file to the PATH command, which will normally be found in the file AUTOEXEC.BAT. Provided you do this and take care to observe any restrictions about where the program's data files should be stored, you should have no trouble running programs from file icons. (It is ironic that a system designed for naive users should require a detailed knowledge of DOS commands to make full use of it, but that's computing for you.)

On some computers, especially IBM and IBM-compatibles, you will be asked if the program needs full memory. GEM takes up a large amount of memory space, and may not leave enough room for large applications on these machines. If you choose the full memory option this will slow down the process of loading and running the program, as GEM has to be cleared from memory. It also slows down the process of returning to GEM after quitting the application, as GEM has to be reloaded (this may involve a degree of disk swapping on a floppy disk based system).

You should choose the full memory option with large applications such as spreadsheets, CAD, and desktop publishing. These programs invariably use large amounts of memory. It may also be advisable to choose this option if you are using a word processor to create large documents, or a database with very large data files. A really powerful word processor, like WordPerfect, Wordstar or Microsoft Word is likely to need full memory anyway. If in doubt, it is safest to select this option.

On GEM 2 and later versions, you can select the form of icons for your application. The icons appear in a window within the dialogue box, and you can scroll through them to find the most appropriate type for your application. It is best in this case to scroll by clicking on the up and down arrows rather than dragging on the scroll bar, as with the latter method it is very easy to skip over icons.

When you have made all your selections, you simply have to click on the Install button to complete the operation (the OK button on version 1 GEM). Click on Cancel if for any reason you decide not to install. On some versions of GEM there is also a Remove button to allow you to un-install a previously installed application.

The installation process takes immediate effect, but only lasts for the current computing session. To make the installation permanent, you must save the Desktop, using the "Save Desktop" option from the OPTIONS menu. Remember that this can alter other aspects of GEM, so make sure everything is as you want it before saving. In particular, set the Desktop windows to the way you want them to appear when GEM is first run.

Running a Non-GEM Application.
With applications which have been correctly installed as DOS-takes parameters, they can be run in two ways, like GEM applications. You can either double-click on a file icon or the program icon, or you can single-click on these icons and then select the "Open" option from the FILES menu. If you select a data file, the program will run and load this file ready for use.

49

If you select a DOS-takes parameters program from the program icon, you will first see a dialogue box titled "Open Application". In this box there will be a line titled "Parameters". You may enter a file name to be loaded, or other parameters taken by the program (see the program manual) on this line, or you may simply click on the "OK" button to run the program without specifying parameters.

With a program which has been installed as a DOS application, you can only run it by double-clicking on the program icon, or single-clicking and using the "Open" option. The program will run immediately, without first displaying a Dialogue box.

It should be mentioned that you do not have to install an application in order to be able to run it from the Desktop. Any application, installed or not, can be run from the program icon. The advantage of installation is that it enables you to select an appropriate pair of icons, and also, on appropriate computers, it enables the selection of the "needs full memory" option. When you run a non-installed application, large parts of GEM remain in memory. If a program has not been installed, it will be assumed to be a DOS-takes parameters type, and the Dialogue box will appear when you run the program. If the program cannot take parameters, you should not type anything in here, as this will cause an error.

Applications which have been installed in GEM can still be run from the DOS prompt if required. Installation only alters GEM. It does not modify the program in any way.

Leaving a Non-GEM Application.
When you have finished with the application, you should use the Quit or Exit option provided by the program. If you simply switch off, this could result in the loss of data, or in some cases could leave redundant temporary files on your disk(s). Most applications will prompt you of any file-saving operations necessary.

Once the application has finished, you will be returned to the Desktop display as it was when you ran the program, or in the case of programs needing full memory with GEM 2, to the initial Desktop display (if working from floppy disks you may need to do some disk swapping). At this display, if you do not intend using the computer further it is safe, after removing any floppy disks from the drive(s), to turn the computer off.

Chapter 5

GEM IN APPLICATIONS PROGRAMS

For programs written to use them, GEM provides a consistent set of facilities for the programmer and the user. Programs written to use these facilities all have a similar look and feel, and once you have learned to use one GEM program, the time taken to learn any other is much reduced. The GEM environment also provides consistent file types from program to program, which makes it easy to swap data between programs. This covers not only data in the conventional sense, but also such things as graphics files.

The Menu Bar.
All GEM programs will feature a menu bar across the top of the screen, just like the Desktop. However, the actual menus on the bar will vary from program to program. Here are some examples.

GEM PAINT.
File Tools Selection Patterns Font Style

Locomotive BASIC 2.
File Program Edit Fonts Colours Patterns Lines Windows

Timeworks DTP
File Edit Options Page Style Text Graphics Help

You can see that although there are major differences between them, there are some things in common. In particular, all programs will have a FILE menu, which will have some options in common on all programs (there may be program-specific options in addition). We will therefore consider this important menu in detail.

The File Menu.
The options which you are likely to find on all FILE menus are:-

Open
Save
Save as...
Abandon (changes)

New
Close
Quit

You will usually also find either "Print" or "To Output" depending on whether the program uses GEM Output (on appropriate machines) or has its own output routine.

"Open" is used to read in a previously created file. It is used to work on an existing piece of work when you have not started the program by clicking on the icon for that file. Some GEM programs allow you to work on more than one job at once. For instance, GEM PAINT allows you to have two drawings in two windows. If you are working on one drawing, and use the "Open" option to load another, the first will not be lost. The new drawing will be placed in the second window. You can move from drawing to drawing by changing windows.

"Save" is used to periodically save your current task to disk. If you are working on a new, untitled piece of work, the first time you use "Save" you will be prompted for a filename. (In this instance "Save" and "Save as..." are effectively the same.) If the work already has a file name, it will be saved using that same name. Depending on the program and (with GEM/3) how GEM is set up, you may be prompted to confirm that you want to overwrite the existing file. It is a good idea to save any work in progress periodically as a precaution against power cuts or other interruptions. The work will remain in memory for further additions or amendments.

"Save as..." allows work in progress to be saved with a new file name. A GEM Item Selector box will appear allowing you to enter the new name. This option can be used to save work to a disk other than the working disk, perhaps for security purposes in case the working disk is corrupted, or because you want to keep a permanent record of some stage of a part-completed work, or because you have made additions or amendments to a finished work, and want to keep the original under its original name. As with "Save", the work will remain in memory. The point to watch here is that the work in memory **retains the original name**. If you subsequently use "Save", your original file will be overwritten.

"Abandon" allows you to abandon any changes made since the work was last saved (it appears as "Abandon changes..." on some menus, especially under GEM/3). You will normally be asked to confirm this action. If the work has never been saved, of course, the whole thing will be lost.

"New" is used to clear the current work from memory. You will normally be asked to confirm this action, and in some programs you will be asked if you want to save before clearing. In the case of programs which allow you to work on two (or more) files at once in different windows, it is the file in the current window which will be cleared. When you clear a file with "New", the window remains open, and remains the current window.

"Close" is similar to "New" in that it clears the current file, and like "New" you are likely to be asked to confirm the action and may be offered the choice of saving before clearing. However, "Close" does close the window which contained the file which was cleared. If there is another window containing a file, it will become the current window. Otherwise, you will be left with no windows open. However, selecting "New" to open a file will automatically open a window. Clicking on the bow-tie symbol has the same effect as "Close". On some programs which only allow work on one document at a time, "Close" is absent as it makes no sense in such a program.

"Quit" is used to exit a program when you have finished working. Normally you will be returned to the GEM Desktop, but in the case of some large GEM programs which can be run direct from the O.S. (such as Timeworks), you may be returned to the O.S. prompt. You should always properly quit a program, not just turn the computer off, as the program may generate temporary files which must be deleted. Having old versions of such files on disk could cause problems next time you use the program, and in any case take up disk space unnecessarily. You may be prompted to save the current work before quitting.

GEM Item Selector.
The GEM Item Selector boxes are about the most consistent thing in the different versions of GEM. They appear whenever you need to open a file or save a file with a new name.

The Item Selector has a number of features, as shown in Figure 17. At the top of the box is a line titled "Directory". In fact, this line indicates the complete path from the current drive to the current folder, in standard O.S. format. The drive letter is separated from the rest of the line by a colon, and the folder name(s) are separated by a ''\'' (not to be confused with ''/''). For example

C:\IMAGES\L__SCAPES*.IMG

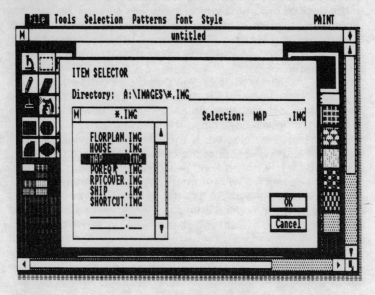

Fig 17. A GEM Item Selector

Below this and to the right is a line marked ''Selection''. It is here that you type in the filename when saving a new file or an existing file with a new name.

To the left is a window in which currently available items are listed. This window has scroll bars so that if there are more items in the current directory than can be listed, you can scroll through them in the normal way. To select an item in this window, you click on it. It will then be highlighted, and will also appear on the ''Selection'' line.

At bottom right there are ''OK'' and ''Cancel'' buttons. You click on the ''OK'' button to proceed with the save or load. The ''Cancel'' button takes you back to whatever you were doing before popping down the FILE menu. Double-clicking on an item in the Directory Window has the same effect as highlighting and then selecting ''OK'', and pressing the Enter key after entering a filename also avoids having to use the "OK" button.

When you select a FILE option, the directory displayed in the Item Selector will be the folder where the program normally expects to store its files (e.g. the Images folder for GEM Paint). To change to a different directory, you must edit the Directory Line. You can do this by clicking on it, which will place a text cursor at the right end of the line. You can then change it with the usual editing keys. You can change as much or as little as you need to, going right back and changing the drive letter if you wish. After finishing the editing, you can press the Enter key if at the right end of the line, or otherwise click on the "OK" button. The contents of the new directory will then appear in the directory window.

If you want to move back a level in the path, you can do so by clicking on the bow-tie symbol in the Directory Window. The Directory Line will change to the new path.

When saving a new file or saving an existing file with a new name, you cannot type the whole of the filename, including the path, in the Directory Line. You must put the actual filename in the Selection line. Suppose, for example, that you are running GEM Paint from drive C, and you want to save a picture to drive A, in a folder called LSCAPES with the filename ALPINE.IMG. On selecting "Save as...", an item selector would appear showing

C:\IMAGES*.*

in the Directory Line, with the Selection line empty. You would first have to edit the Directory line by deleting everything in it, and then typing

A:\LSCAPES\

Alternatively, you could just type the drive identifier (including the colon) and then select the folder from the Directory window. You would then type ALPINE.IMG in the Selection line and either press Enter or click on the "OK" button to complete the save operation.

In fact, it is only necessary to type the simple filename (in this case ALPINE), as the program will add the appropriate extension automatically. If you specify a different extension, in many GEM programs it will be overridden. Filename extensions are a vital part of GEM and should not normally be changed.

When you move through the file structure by selecting folders in the Directory window, the Directory line will change and the contents of the new folder will be displayed in the Directory window. However, sometimes, when you reach a level where there are no further folders within the folder selected, the files in that folder are not displayed, the Directory window remaining empty. To cause the files to be displayed, you must add the wildcard "*" to the end of the path in the Directory line. It must be followed by a full stop and either another "*", to display all files, or the valid filename extension for the program, to display those files only. If you then click on "OK" or press Enter, the files should be displayed.

In general, if you do not put a wildcard after the last folder name, only folders within the folder will be displayed. If you put *.EXT, folders and files with the extension EXT will be displayed (EXT is used here to represent the required extension for your purpose), and if you put *.*, all files in the folder will be displayed. Some programs do seem to vary this slightly, however.

Fonts.

Most GEM programs which allow text entry (and that is most programs) provide a selection of fonts in which text can be displayed.

A font is not just a style of text. Each size in a given style is a different font, so to specify a font it requires both a style and a size.

Normally, GEM provides three styles as standard. These are the System style, which is the one built into the computer, Swiss, which is a sans serif style loosely based on Helvetica, and Dutch, a serified style based, again loosely, on Times Roman. Each of these styles is available in a number of sizes.

Text sizes are specified in points. In GEM, a point is 1/72in., and the height of a character is used to specify its size, so a 36 point capital letter would be one half-inch high. This applies both to the screen and the printer, provided GEM has been correctly set up for your equipment.

The number of sizes you can use will vary according to your computer and the version of GEM you are using. On the two machines the Author uses, system style is available in 8,10,16 and 20 point, but on one Swiss and Dutch are available in

10,14,18,20,28 and 36 point, while on the other they are available in 7 and 72 points in addition. This applies to the screen fonts. Printer fonts are often not available in sizes over 28 point, depending on the type of printer you use. Laser printers are generally more accommodating than dot-matrix types (daisy-wheel or thimble type printers cannot of course be used to print GEM fonts). Figure 18 shows some of the fonts available in the Author's installation of GEM Paint.

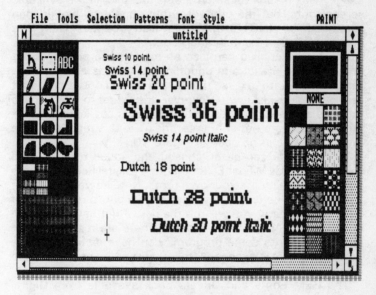

Fig 18. A Selection of GEM Fonts

The distinction between screen and printer fonts is an important one. The patterns stored in memory for the two are quite different. This allows for the fact that the resolution which a dot-matrix printer — even a nine-pin type — can manage is considerably higher than is possible on even the best screen displays. The printer fonts must of course be the correct ones for your printer. For GEM 2, default fonts for Epson FX compatible printers are built-in, and a "GEM Fonts and Drivers Pack" is available from Digital Research. This has fonts for many popular printers including 24-pin, laser and some colour printers, and also some pen plotters. GEM/3 is supplied with drivers for a wide range of printers. On a hard disk installation, up to four printers can be installed.

The printer fonts are used by GEM applications like GEM Draw and Wordchart which produce files with the .GEM extension, and also by GEM based word processors which use similar types of file but may use a .DOC or .TXT extension. Programs like GEM Paint which produce .IMG files do not use the printer fonts as their output is derived from the screen image. This means these programs can use all the available screen fonts, but the printed output cannot be higher than screen quality. (NOTE: GEM Paint also produces .GEM files but these do not contain image data.)

The fonts supplied can also be modified to provide light, bold, skewed (italic) and underlined text. It is also possible for GEM to rotate text, so that it runs up and down the page, or is printed upside down. However, the extent to which these facilities are used depends on the particular application. Some programmers are not very enterprising in this regard. (Some inverted text can be seen in Figure 10.)

Further fonts can be purchased and added to GEM, and there is also a GEM Font Editor program (Digital Research) with which you can create your own fonts. Note however that the fonts have to be loaded into memory as part of GEM, and if you add too many you will run the risk of not having enough memory left for your applications. There are restrictions on how many fonts some programs can have installed at one time, and if this is exceeded, menu corruption and other side effects may result.

The GEM Fonts and Drivers pack available from Digital Research, mentioned above is strictly a set of printer and plotter drivers, and the fonts referred to in the name are for these printers and plotters. This pack does not add any additional fonts to GEM applications.

Once fonts are added, they can generally be used by all appropriate GEM programs. However, some programs can only use a restricted range of fonts, probably because of memory constraints. One desktop publishing program used by the Author can only use the Swiss and Dutch fonts in 7,10,14,20,28 and 36 point with dot-matrix printers, though a very wide range is available with some laser printers.

File Types.
GEM applications save data in specific file types, the format

of which is consistent from program to program. It is this which makes it possible for files generated by one program to be used by another, provided it is designed to do so. Thus, a GEM-based word processor like First Word Plus can read in image files created by GEM Paint and include graphics in documents.

This facility is particularly useful in desk top publishing, for which GEM is now very widely used. These programs rely on the ability to mix text and various forms of graphics.

There are two distinct types of graphics data files used by GEM programs. Programs like GEM Paint which are screen-drawing programs, and pixel based, save screen images in files with the extension .IMG. This type of file is termed ''pixel orientated''. The amount of detail in these images can never be higher than that of the screen on which they are drawn. Detail can, however, be lost if the image is subsequently edited on a screen with a lower resolution.

Programs like GEM Draw and GEM Wordchart do not store pixel images. The files they store are a description of each element of the image. This type of file is usually termed ''object orientated''. The extension .GEM is used for this type of file. When this type of file is output on another device, such as a printer, the text is formed using the printer fonts, and the graphics are recreated on the printer. A considerably better quality of output is possible than from pixel-orientated programs.

The files from some GEM word processors are similar to the .GEM type in that they contain the text with a description of the fonts used, and the printer fonts are used when printing the document, ensuring the highest possible quality of output.

The filename extensions are used by GEM to identify the appropriate type of file, and, where both .IMG and .GEM files can be used, to make sure the data is correctly processed during the input process. You should never change these file extensions, as if you do so, programs will refuse to read them. You should also not use these extensions for non-GEM files, though there are safety precautions included in the files and programs to prevent an inappropriate file with one of these extensions from crashing a GEM application.

Chapter 6

GEM OUTPUT

GEM Output is a GEM application program used with versions of GEM running under MS-DOS, PC-DOS and similar operating systems. It is used for producing printed output on printers and pen plotters, and can also send output to the screen without the usual window borders of GEM programs, for display purposes. In fact, it can be set to cycle through a number of screen images, and this can be used for exhibition or shop window displays. Output can also be sent to a camera device to produce colour slides or colour or black-and-white prints of screen images.

GEM Output is not used on the Atari ST implementation of GEM, or on some other GEM 1 installations. For these, each program must have its own output facility. This explains why some programs originally written for the Atari STs and then converted for other computers do not use Output.

Some GEM applications do not in any case use Output. This may be the way the program works. This is particularly true of desk top publishing programs, where the output facilities are very much integrated into the program design. Locomotive BASIC 2, the programming language supplied with the Amstrad PC computers, also does not use Output, as it can itself direct output to any device fixed to the computer.

Some word processors running under GEM may be able to either output directly or generate a file for use with GEM Output. With these, the in-built routine is usually a rapid draft mode, which uses the printer's fonts. Printing via Output will be slower but will be able to use the full range of GEM fonts and features.

The two versions of Output used by versions 2 and 3 of GEM have significant differences, which will be described as they occur, but the first step in using them, creating an output list, is substantially the same for both.

Creating an Output List.
You cannot simply specify a file to be printed by Output. The name of the file must first be placed on an output list, and it is the list that is specified in the Output program. If you just

want to output one file, the simplest way is to go to Output direct from the application in which the file is loaded. An output list containing this single item will be produced automatically. To do this, click on "To Output..." on the FILE menu.

In all other cases, you must first make an output list. This is done within the Output application, so you must first run this from the Desktop.

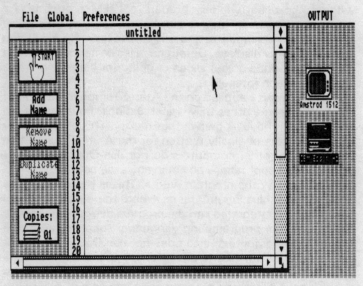

Fig 19. GEM 3 Output Initial Screen

When the program starts, you will see an empty output list in the middle of the screen. Figure 19 shows the initial screen of GEM/3 Output. To add names to this list, pop down the EDIT menu and select "Add Name". This will produce a GEM Item Selector box which you can use in the usual way (see Chapter 5) to select items. When you click on the "OK" button in the Item Selector, the selected item is added to the output list. Note that all items in an output list must be in the same folder, but you may mix file types (e.g. .GEM files, .IMG files) in a list.

There is a short cut you can use to build up a list quickly.

If you click on the "OK" button without either highlighting any item or entering anything into the Selection line, all the names in the current window will be added.

You may have noted that programs like GEM Paint produce both .IMG and .GEM files for each picture. Though it is the .IMG file which contains the data for printing, it is the .GEM file which will be placed on the output list (even if you select the .IMG file on the Item Selector). Both must be present for Output to print the file.

Each output list may contain up to 36 names. However, it is not a good idea to produce too long a list, because of the time it will take to print. It is not a good idea to leave a printer unattended for too long, as paper jams and other problems can and do occur. This does not apply, of course, to sending sequences of images to the screen.

If you want to remove a name from an output list, you can do this by means of the "Remove Name" option on the EDIT menu. Once you have finished your output list, you can save it in case you want to output the same set of files again at some time in the future. This is especially valuable with sets of screen images.

Output gives the option of printing one, two or more copies of every item in the output list. If you want extra copies of one or a few items in the list, you can simply repeat the name in the list. Again, this can be useful with sequences of screen images.

Once the output list is complete, you can start Output immediately. However, there is a bug in some versions of GEM 2 output where if you have created and saved a list, and immediately try to use it, you will be told it is the wrong type of file, and Output can only open files of type .LIS? The answer is simply to quit Output, and restart it by double clicking on the output list icon from the Desktop.

Printer Options.
Selecting "Printer" from the OPTIONS menu ("Page" on the PREFERENCES menu on version 3) allows you to set up how the output will be sized and placed on the paper, and other aspects of printer control. It is substantially the same for the GEM 2 and 3 versions, but the screen presentation is different. Figure 20 shows the GEM 2 screen.

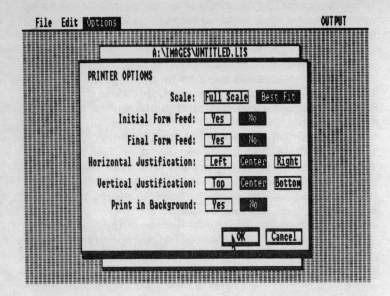

A:\IMAGES\UNTITLED.LIS

PRINTER OPTIONS

Scale: **Full Scale** Best Fit

Initial Form Feed: Yes No

Final Form Feed: Yes No

Horizontal Justification: Left Center **Right**

Vertical Justification: Top Center **Bottom**

Print in Background: Yes No

OK Cancel

Fig 20. GEM 2 Output Printer Options

Firstly, you can choose the size of output. You can either print
at full scale (true scale in vsn.3), which will print a drawing
at the size at which it was drawn (i.e. screen size), provided
the paper size on your printer is big enough, or it can be printed
at ''best fit'', (or ''make fit'' on vsn. 3), which will scale the
image up or down to fit the paper. Version 2 assumes a paper
size of 8.5 x 11 inches. Version 3 allows selection of paper
sizes (see foreword).Scaling will always be proportionate, so
the image will only fit the paper one way, unless the paper
proportions match the proportions of the image.

You can choose whether to send an initial form feed and
a final form feed to your printer. Form feeds cause the printer
to move to the start of a new sheet, and are appropriate only
to printers using continuous stationery or sheet feeders. Normally you would only want to send one or the other. If your
printer runs a sequence of images together, so that the images
run over the perforations between sheets, you need to add
a form feed. If, on the other hand, it shoots out a blank sheet
of paper between each pair of printed sheets, you need to

cancel a form feed. (Version 3 Output has only a final form feed option. It cannot send an initial form feed, and release 3.01 cannot send a final form feed either, so this option is inoperative.)

You can select how to place the output on the paper. The image can be justified left or right or centred in the horizontal direction, or justified top or bottom or centred in the vertical direction. In version 2 the selection is made by clicking on buttons. In version 3 it is done by graphical representation, clicking at the edges or in the centre of the icon. Figure 21 shows the GEM/3 screen display. Of course, if you have chosen the best fit/make fit option, placement can only be effective in one direction, or not at all if the proportions match.

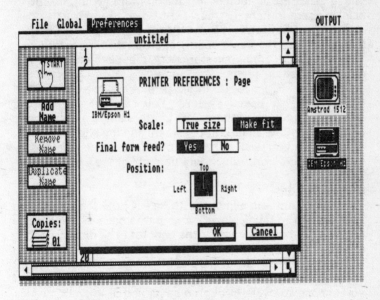

Fig 21. GEM 3 Output Printer Preferences

On version 2, you have the option of background printing. This means that after Output has started printing, control of the computer will return to the Desktop, and further programs can be run while printing continues. However, this slows both the program and the printing, and is only really practical on the most powerful computers. A minimum of 320K of memory is required. This feature has been deleted on version 3.

On version 3, the PREFERENCES — "Paper" option allows you to set the paper size you are using. The available sizes are:-

HALF	8.5 x 5.5
LETTER	8.5 x 11
LEGAL	8.5 x 14
LEDGER	11 x 17
BROAD	18 x 24
WIDE	14 x 11
A4	8.27 x 11.69
B5	7.17 x 9.84

These sizes are in inches. In the program, you can opt to display them in centimetres.

With the PREFERENCES — "Paper tray" option (GEM/3), you can select the paper supply appropriate for your printer. You can select continuous stationery, manual feed, or various options for sheet feeders.

On version 3, up to 4 printers or plotters can be installed on a hard disk based system. You can set the options separately for each of them. The printers are shown as icons on the right of the initial output screen, and the one to be used, or for which you wish to set the options, can be selected by clicking on its icon, which will be highlighted.

Screen Options.
The screen options allow you to select how long you wish each picture to be displayed, and, in the case of a sequence of images, whether you want the print list to be displayed once only, or cycled repeatedly.

You can choose to display each image for 2,5,10 or 20 seconds, or until a key (or the mouse button) is pressed. If you choose to cycle through a sequence of images, no tidy way to end the output is provided. You have to reset the computer with the ctrl\alt\del key combination. Figure 22 shows the Screen Options display for GEM 2 Output, and the GEM/3 version is essentially similar.

Camera Options.
The camera options allow you to set the type of film which will be used in the camera device. Note that these options are

only relevant to a camera device connected to the computer, not to photographing the screen with an ordinary camera. There is a choice of conventional colour or black-and-white film, or of several Polaroid instant materials.

Plotter Options.
Plotter options are very similar to the printer options, and are selected and used in the same way.

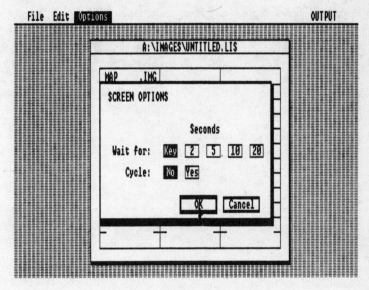

Fig 22. GEM 2 Output Screen Options

Index

N.B. Page numbers in *italics* refer to illustrations.

NOTES

NOTES